HONOR
& DEMISE

(A True Story)

BY

Diane Simpson

The contents of this work, including, but not limited to, the accuracy of events, people, and places depicted; opinions expressed; permission to use previously published materials included; and any advice given or actions advocated are solely the responsibility of the author, who assumes all liability for said work and indemnifies the publisher against any claims stemming from publication of the work.

All Rights Reserved
Copyright © 2017 by Diane Simpson

No part of this book may be reproduced or transmitted, downloaded, distributed, reverse engineered, or stored in or introduced into any information storage and retrieval system, in any form or by any means, including photocopying and recording, whether electronic or mechanical, now known or hereinafter invented without permission in writing from the publisher.

Dorrance Publishing Co
585 Alpha Drive
Suite 103
Pittsburgh, PA 15238
Visit our website at *www.dorrancebookstore.com*

ISBN: 978-1-4809-3585-3
eISBN: 978-1-4809-3562-4

I would like to dedicate this book to all of our family and friends who are no longer with us.

HONOR & DEMISE

I always had a feeling I was going to lose one of my children.

I believe when we lose our loved ones, they will always be with us in spirit and in our hearts. If we are lucky enough we will witness our loved ones communicating with what I like to call "angel signs."

Like my mother before me, I have witnessed angel signs. Whether it be in dreams, or seeing them in person, signs of angels are all around us—showing us God's presence is all around us—we just need to be aware of our surroundings.

The story you are about to read is true. Amazingly enough, I have photos to confirm our sightings of angel signs. My mother planted the seed of faith in her children. She was a very wonderful, good Christian woman. Her faith was strong and she encouraged us to be the same way. For planting that seed in me, I am very grateful.

If you are a nonbeliever, my hope is after you read this story you will believe in the love of our savior Jesus Christ. He is the love, hope, and joy for all mankind. We are blessed in so many ways, especially to have everlasting life, what a gift.

As my story begins, my mother was at the hospital with me because I was running a high fever and coughing. I was an infant at the time, just weeks old. As it turned out, I had pneumonia. The doctors had done all they could possibly do to help me. They had told Mom that there was nothing more they could do.

Stricken with grief, my mother could not sleep that night. She tossed and turned, finally her eyes closed, and she fell asleep. She awoke with a gentle touch, and when she opened her eyes she saw her father at the foot of her bed.

"Margie," he said, "I come to you as a messenger from heaven, do not worry about Diane. She is going to make it, she will be just fine." With that his glowing appearance went away.

Mom, stunned but hopeful, couldn't believe what just happened. Was it a dream or did this really happen? Did she see her dad? Was Diane going to be okay?

A few days later the doctor came to Mom and said to her, "Diane is going to be okay." The doctor then stated, "It was nothing we did, this came from a higher power." As he pointed his finger upward to heaven, Mom knew right then that God had sent her dad to deliver the good news, that they were watching over mom and me.

My grandfather was killed in a motor vehicle accident while he was home on leave from the army. My mother was six months pregnant with me. I was always told my grandfather was a wonderful man.

We all have some tragedies in life, but we also have blessings. We need to live each day to our best and always remember, as the saying goes, God never gives us more than we can handle.

Five years later, my sisters Judy and Sandy, now in heaven, were with us at home. Mom was at work and they were watching me and my other sisters Millie, Cindy, and Linda. We had just finished lunch, and they had asked us if we wanted to go outside and play or take a nap. I felt very tired so I chose to take a nap. When I woke up, I could not move my legs. I screamed and my sisters came running. They called an ambulance. I remember this wool grey blanket the EMTs put on me. I was so scared and was crying and yelling. I could not figure out what was wrong with me and why they put a wool blanket on me on such a warm day.

We found out the paralysis in my legs was from rheumatic fever. Treatment for this illness was penicillin injections for years, once a month, right after school.

My paralysis lasted a year and confined me to a wheelchair. My brother Richard used to push me really fast in it, which I loved. What I didn't love was the physical therapy—holding onto those bars, moving my legs. It hurt so much trying to walk again, I don't know what was worse, therapy or receiving those injections. They burned so bad, but the shots were only once a month. A homecare nurse would always be there when I came home from school, four o'clock sharp. I always hoped she would not be there, but she always was. Therapy seemed like it was never ending, but by God's grace I did walk again. My second angel in my life had watched over me.

As an adult, I have Mitral Valve Regurgitation from the rheumatic fever. It is not severe and I keep an eye on it.

It has been fifty-five years since my illness. I feel very healthy and am so blessed for my family and friends. I don't take anything for granted anymore. I try to make the best out of each and every day, always think positively, and love all the people in my life.

Years later, I got married and started a family. I was blessed to have two healthy boys. My oldest son Tim had some health issues as an infant, but nothing life threatening. Dan, my youngest, and Tim were only thirteen months apart. They grew up to be very close.

As it happens with some marriages, ours did not last. The boys were seven and eight years old when ours ended.

As a single parent raising two boys, I don't know if I had a sixth sense or if I was overly protective of them, but I got the feeling that I was going to lose one of my children. When Dan was a young teenager, he started smoking pot and drinking beer. He struggled through most of his teenage years and on into adulthood.

Counseling and multiple stints in rehab many times didn't seem to help. At the age of sixteen, Dan seemed to be doing better. During this time, I met a man named Ken. He was a good man and we hit it off right away.

One New Year's Eve, he told me that he wanted our relationship to go to the next level. We had a long talk. I wanted to see what his religious beliefs were so I asked Ken if he believed in God. His response was, "I believe in a higher power, I don't know if that is God." Then he started talking about science and atoms, things of which I had no concept.

We talked until about four in the morning. I made it very clear several times if he did not believe in God, we could not have a relationship. Finally, he admitted that he believed. We continued to see each other. Just over a week later, on January 8th, Ken took us out to celebrate Dan's 17th birthday. Dan, Tim, one of Dan's good friends Derrick, and I were there. We all had a wonderful time. Little did Tim, Dan, or Derrick know that was the last time they would see Ken. Four days later I was at Ken's house having dinner with him. After dinner, Ken and I were talking downstairs. I was sitting in a chair, reading a book. I looked up at Ken to tell him something, but received no response. He was lying on the couch. I moved closer and heard a gurgling sound and saw that he was not breathing. I called 911. When the ambulance got there, they asked me to go upstairs. I was so nervous and scared. It turned out they were giving him CPR with no success; they knew he was gone but tried to bring him back. They then rushed him to the hospital, but it was too late. Ken had passed away of a sudden heart attack.

That experience of talking to someone one minute, and having them gone the next minute is one I would never want to happen again.

A few days later, I wondered if Ken truly believed in God or if that New Year's Eve he just told me he believed just to shut me up. It was late—four o'clock in the morning—he must have been tired and wanted some sleep.

I worried about that while I was at his house, waiting for his mom and brother to get there from California. I prayed, "God, I sure do hope Ken is with you in heaven."

I was sitting in the dark having a cigarette when I saw what appeared to be a bouncing ball floating in the air. I looked closer and saw it was Ken's smiling face. I saw his face five or six times and then it disappeared. When I told his mother about this, she thought it must have been a dream. I would have thought so too, but I know I was wide awake because I was smoking a cigarette.

This was another one of God's angels taking care of me. At that time I was a cigarette smoker and had tried many times to quit. I decided to try to quit smoking again. I stopped cold turkey on my sister Linda's birthday—March 18th—I quit, never to put another cigarette in my mouth again. I am now twenty-three years smoke free.

There is always a time for everything, keep trying for your goals, and never give up. I think Ken would have been very happy I quit smoking. In fact, I think he knows.

Over the next few years, Dan still struggled with his addiction to drugs and alcohol. I constantly worried that he would overdose, get killed, or commit suicide. He just did not listen to anyone. While Dan was going down this dangerous path, Tim moved to Arizona to go to school. He wanted to be a graphic arts designer, so he was attending the Al Collins School of Graphic Arts in Tempe, Arizona.

Meanwhile, Dan continued falling off the wagon. Police had come to my house to tell me Dan was in the ER and had been found lying on the ground. "Dan," I told him, "you have got to stop this behavior, you have been doing this for too long—it has been years now, you have children now, you have to think about them. You cannot continue this lifestyle."

Tim called me from Arizona. "Mom," he said, "it's pretty rough working and going to school and paying for it all. I have decided to join the Army, they will pay for my schooling." So Tim joined the Army, he began traveling everywhere, and loved it so much he re-enlisted.

Dan struggled. He was having ups and downs with his addictions; he would fall off the wagon, and then he would do really well. It didn't help that he had enablers in his life. I just felt helpless and hurt, scared something was going to happen to him. Dan was now in his late twenties, and I prayed his life would turn around for good—not just for periods of time—his children were growing up fast.

I gave Dan my airline ticket to attend his brother's wedding, Tim had met his girlfriend two years before. They had planned on getting married anyway, but they decided to get married before the possibility of Tim being sent overseas, so that she could come with him. I had thought it might help Dan to see his brother so Tim could talk to him, brother to brother. It worked for a while, and Dan made other trips to see Tim in Georgia with his children, Taylor and Cheyenne. They loved seeing their Uncle Tim and also loved the beach. To this day Cheyenne wants to live in Georgia.

Tim knew about Dan's struggles and his trips and in out of rehab, never finishing a program. He offered Dan the opportunity to come and stay with him for a while and Dan accepted.

It wasn't like Dan had many offers at home, he had just lost a job, which was one of many jobs he had lost in the past. He burned about every bridge with his family and what close, decent friends he had, including his AA sponsor.

Tim was always a good role model for Dan and I knew it would do him some good to spend time with his brother. Tim, still in the service, suggested that Dan join the Army also. Dan was seriously thinking about it. I tried to encourage him to join. The Army would offer him so many opportunities and give him a secure future. He decided against it, and I wish he had not changed his mind.

He returned home after Tim's deployment. Let's just say he did not do well while Tim was gone. He had decided to come back home. I'm sure he wanted to be with his children more than just summers and other short visits when possible, and some people cannot handle military life, as was the case with Tim's wife. She did not like the uprooting from home to home. Needless to say, their marriage was short-lived.

Dan came home to be with his children and his on-again, off-again girlfriend, who is also the mother of his children. Things were going pretty well for a while, then, as always, they went back to that cycle of dysfunction. They are toxic together. I just knew someday something bad was going to happen, I just hoped it would not be the deep feeling I've had for many years that I was going to lose my son. Their lifestyle was so bad for the kids. They knew they would always have me. Even though they have not had the best family life, they have grown up to be amazing.

I received a call from Tim from Hinesville, Georgia at Fort Stewart. He tells me, "Mom, you are not going to hear from me for a while. I can't tell you where I am going or what I'm doing, I don't want you to worry but I will not be able to communicate in the states for a while. I will tell you though, something big is going to happen." Days later, on television, I saw a special news report that read "U.S. Military forces invading Baghdad, April 9th, 2003."

I knew at that moment Tim was in Baghdad. When they said it was the 3rd infantry division and that they were bombing, I knew. Tim was with the 3rd infantry division air defense artillery.

Tim traveled to many places in his years of military service with the United States Army, including Turkey, Germany, France, Italy, Jerusalem and Amsterdam. He assisted in the California wildfires. He was sent on three tours in Iraq.

With Operation Iraqi Freedom, Tim was deployed to two more tours, as Iraq had become a war zone. Therefore, not only was I worrying about Dan, but I was also worried about Tim being in harm's way. His first tour in Iraq was safe, and he was safe. On Tim's second tour, things were different, and I prayed he would come home safe just as I continued to pray for Dan to change his life around. Dan had a good heart, attended church regularly, but just hadn't given himself completely to God. I hoped someday he would.

Tim's second tour in Iraq ended and he came home safely. Thank you, God.

I was still worrying about Dan, he was doing better and not having as many intoxicated nights, but he still had a long way to go.

It was nice that Tim was back in the states. When he would call and ask how Dan was doing, I would tell him that he was doing better. Tim never knew if Dan was being completely honest with him.

Tim came home on leave, and it was good for both of them to spend time together. When Tim was in the states, he either came home to us or we would go to him. We always enjoyed each other and had very happy times visiting and sightseeing new places we had never been to before.

Tim had decided to leave active military duty. He went to the US Army Aviation Logistics School, graduated and joined the Arizona Army National Guard at the Papago Park Military Reservation in Phoenix, Arizona. He worked as an aviation mechanic, working on Blackhawk helicopters and went on to be a Blackhawk crew chief.

He loved his job and loved to fly, with Sergeant First Class Michael Ness and the 285th Aviation Battalion at Papago Park. The 285th battalion are great to work with. They are good people. Tim loved his new job and I was happy he had stateside military duty instead of active duty. He was safer in the states, and out of harm's way.

Tim's unit in Arizona got ready to go to Fort Sill in Oklahoma, for military duty in Iraq. This was his third deployment. He never expected to be deployed again to Iraq. The deployment which was in 2009 reached national attention on television and newspaper, and a video of the takeoff of the ten Blackhawk helicopters leaving for Fort Sill to meet other soldiers that were also going to Iraq. The video is awesome, I saw it on my computer at home.

Tim later told me he was in the third helicopter, with the 285th Aviation Battalion.

The unit was gone for a year. Back home, I was looking at photos I took just before Tim was deployed, he was so very proud to be in the military and to be a crew chief.

Tim was good about bringing me home souvenirs from places he has been from in his military travels. I have souvenirs from France, Germany, Amsterdam, Italy, and Jerusalem.

Dan was doing much better. He was reconnecting with his church Men's Group and attending church regularly, taking his children with him.

Our family was finally feeling normal again. There had been many times I would stress out when Dan called me. I would wonder what he had gotten himself into now or if he wanted money because he blew of all of his money on drugs and alcohol? I was beginning to feel relaxed during his phone calls to me, they weren't the calls I used to get from him.

Dan was baptized and very involved in church functions, it was a very good feeling. I was so happy for him.

Tim called me on Mother's Day like he always had in the past. He never remembered my birthday. Dan always reminded him of the date. On that phone call, he said he was coming home for Christmas, which was great. His unit had just gotten back from a three week assignment in Panama, South America.

Things were great, and I was beginning to wonder if that feeling I've had for so long was not true. My woman's intuition—that feeling I had about losing one of my children—was fading away, and I had not thought about that in a very long time.

One day I was at home getting ready for work, and when I picked up my cell phone, I noticed that the power charge was very low. So I left my phone at home to charge up. I thought no one would call me, because everyone knew I was working that day. There was a time when I would never leave my phone at home. That day I'm glad I did. It was another angel looking out for me.

We were very busy at work. I finally was able to get lunch at two o'clock, and was scheduled to get off at 3:30 P.M.

"Diane, you have an emergency phone call," Debbie, my coworker, told me.

When I said hello, my son Dan was on the other end. My first thought was that it was Dan and his girlfriend arguing again and the police were called again for domestic issues. I knew it was too good to be true; they had a good run with no major issues in their lives.

I say, "Now what? What's going on with you guys?" Dan says, "We're okay," then I started to panic, especially when he started crying. I asked him to tell me what was wrong. He says meet me, I don't want to talk on the phone. I am nervous and anxious.

"Oh my God, it's one of the kids, what happened?"

Dan, still crying, said, "No, Mom, it's Tim, he's in trouble."

I thought, "What? In trouble? Tim?" I told Dan I was on my way. My coworkers asked me what was wrong. I told them that I wasn't sure, but that Dan had said I had to talk to him about Tim in Arizona.

I left work to meet Dan, I was nervous, thinking that whole time that Tim was in trouble. My thoughts were police trouble, but that couldn't be right. I couldn't figure out what it could be, or why was Dan crying. I saw Dan standing, pacing on the sidewalk. I pull up, Dan gets in the car and I park the car in the lot of Grady's Pizza parlor.

I turn to Dan, nervously and asked him if Tim was in trouble, and what he did.

"No, Mom, Dan says Tim is not in trouble. He's gone."

"What do you mean by gone?"

"Mom, there was a stabbing, a guy stabbed Tim and another guy, Tim did not survive, he died."

"What, Dan? Quit lying to me!"

Dan looked at me and shook his head no and I was shaking so much, Dan hugged me I hugged him so hard, we were both crying so hard, it seemed like an eternity before we stopped crying.

I asked Dan if he contacted his father and he said he had texted him but had not heard anything. "I was afraid to tell you Mom, that's why I said on the phone that Tim was in trouble, I could not tell you news like that over the phone."

Dan said a detective had called him because he had found his number in Tim's cell phone, which a friend of Tim's, Pete, used to call 911 and the police. He had tried calling me, but of course my phone was at home. I'm so thankful I did not get the news on the phone at work. Dan told me that the detective would give me a call that night.

We went back to my house to begin making phone calls.

The weather was starting to be windy and nasty, and tornado watches were issued. Dan called his kids, and told them to come over to their Grandma's house right away, his voice shaky and demanding. The girls Taylor and Cheyenne were home alone, which was no big deal, as they were old enough to be home alone. Cheyenne, Dan's daughter called me and asked if I wanted them to come over right away due to the tornado watches. She knew it was urgent by the way her dad was acting, and she thought a tornado was coming their way and that we wanted them to take cover with us.

I told her that I just needed them to come over right away and that it was very important. We wanted them not to hear the news until they could hear it from us. Shortly after they arrived, Jerry, Dan's dad, Dan's son and Dan's girlfriend arrived. We needed to tell them in person also.

Reality was hitting me more and more. Tim was gone, he was dead. I realized then that the feeling I'd always had about losing a child had finally come true. Word was getting around about Tim and my house was filled with family, friends, and coworkers. Everyone was so generous, bringing food and their love and support. We all couldn't believe Tim served tours in harm's way without a scratch on him just to come home and get murdered.

I spoke to Detective Brown, who was such a nice lady. She was on the phone with me for an hour and we had a very hard conversation. It was hard to hear what happened to my son. Thankfully there were witnesses and the person responsible was arrested and in jail with an $800,000 bond. He was not going anywhere but jail, and once he was tried in a court of law, prison. She told me how this man came into this apartment and just started stabbing men. Two men were stabbed, my son and another man. The other man didn't sustain life-threatening injuries. He stabbed Tim near the liver, Tim had run out of the apartment to his apartment in the complex. Nearby, Tim's friend saw him, and he held pressure to Tim's wound and called 911. Detective Brown says they tried to save Tim's life, gave him eight pints of blood, he bled out, he died in surgery, there was too much damage to his liver.

In Arizona, Pete and Dan had been keeping in touch. I was so thankful that Pete was nearby and helped Tim, I am grateful that Tim knew that help was on the way.

Pete contacted Tim's military unit, to let them know what happened, which started the beginning of many angels that came to us to help comfort us, the many signs we saw to let us know Tim is still with us. Not only do we have memories of Tim, we have real signs that Tim communicated with us. We have photos of these miracle sightings.

I couldn't sleep, my family stayed with me, and I tried calling Tim, realized what I was doing, and thought I was going crazy. He was not going to answer, what was I doing? I had spoken to Tim on Mother's Day and three days prior to this horrible tragedy—May 30th, 2013.

I had moved into a condo Tim bought for me two years earlier. I couldn't wait for Tim to be home for Christmas to see what I had done to make home improvements on my condo. I moved into the condo, not knowing he would never see those home improvements.

I called Tim again, what am I doing, this is the second time I had called Tim that day. Am I going to lose it? Shortly after, I received a phone call from Arizona, which made me feel better. It was Tim's unit sending their condolences and speaking very highly of Tim, or "Timmy", as they called him. They loved him. Sergeant Michael Ness told me that he was not only Timmy's Sergeant but a very close friend and that Timmy had been a visitor to his home many times. He wanted me to know that the unit was not only friends to me and my family, but family who will never go away. He kept his word, and we did go through a lot together the next couple of years. He has helped so much.

It had been two days since Tim passed, and I hadn't slept, eaten, or showered. I kept praying to God, telling God that Tim was such a good person, loved everyone, so generous, humble, and kind; that he could not have been more of the ideal person that God wants us all to be. I prayed that God please give me a sign that Tim is in heaven.

It was the third day since Tim has passed. It was five o'clock in the morning and I had been up all night, crying and praying. People were calling me the last couple of days, but I didn't want to talk to anyone besides Dan and the kids. I wanted to call Tim again, but I know he would not answer. If only I could talk to him one more time. I was sure his phone was disconnected by now anyway. I decided to delete his phone number from my contact list on my phone. I didn't want to accidentally call him again.

Just like Tim's unit in Phoenix, Arizona, his previous unit—3rd infantry air defense artillery—had a special connection with Tim. They nicknamed him "Turtle" when they were deployed, Tim with his army gear on his back, looked like a turtle with his small neck and head. Tim was a small guy. Tim cherished the name Turtle. Dan did not know this nor did I. Dan had bought Tim a t-shirt with a turtle on it when he was staying with him in Hinesville, Georgia. He spoke of Tim always wearing that t-shirt, he would wash it and wear it again the next day. Now, whenever I hear the word turtle, I think of Tim and smile.

Sergeant Ness had told me to keep my phone close by, he said I would be getting several phone calls. He was so right, it was very overwhelming. I did call the unit trying to locate Sergeant Ness. I did get a call from him and he assured me that we were going to plan Tim's funeral together and we'd get him back home for his service. He would be my go-to guy and he gave me his phone number. It was so nice to talk to one person about all of this instead of multiple people—a lot less stressful. I had told Sergeant Ness, I wanted to honor Tim and give a beautiful military send-off.

He loved being in the service and he would be so happy with the send-off I was planning.

With phone calls to the funeral home in Arizona and back home, we arranged to have Tim's body flown home. Still praying, asking God if Tim was with him in heaven, I got upset and prayed to God: "your son Jesus rose from the grave three days after he died, you are late, this is the fourth day, please show me a sign that Tim is with you." There was a knock at the door, it was late Sunday morning. I answered the door, it is Dan. He told me after church service a picture came on the big screen overhead, Pastor Mike Baker had told the congregation he felt it in his heart to show this picture. Pastor Baker or Dan not knowing I was praying for a sign. I started crying and told Dan, that is my sign, that I had been praying for God to show me a sign and he did. On the big screen was Jesus, a young man kneeling before him, Jesus holding him in his arms with an angel behind them with a white robe. I felt so blessed and happy, I knew Tim was with Jesus in heaven.

I keep my phone close by, Tim is on his way home, the funeral director told us we will have a private viewing of Tim before the visitation. My phone rings, I think it's the funeral home, I say hello but no one answers, I look at the phone and it is all black, I must have accidentally hung up or it was the wrong number.

I felt comfort now, I get the photos now for Tim's service—there is going to be a viewing of forty photos at Tim's service and visitation. We chose photos of some of our happiest memories of Tim and the trips we have taken and of course Tim's favorites. Tim loved sailing, so we had to use a photo of that for sure. We used a photo of him with an army buddy and his brother on the sailboat on the Atlantic Ocean in Georgia. Photos of his nieces with him on the beach. Myself and Tim on the beach with Dan at Hilton Head, South Carolina. Photos of Dan, Tim, and I at Tybee Island climbing the stairs up the lighthouse. Wonderful memories. Georgia Water Street was amazing, horse drawn carriages. We really enjoyed Savannah Smiles, it was a piano bar we went to. The two young men were awesome, they did know every word to every song they sang while playing the piano.

There was also on the video, pictures of Tim with his military friends overseas, and last but not least, close family photos—ranging from birth to adulthood.

I take the photos to the funeral director, and she told me Tim is going to be on a plane which is going to land in Missouri, the funeral home will pick him up. She scheduled our first viewing of Tim. I was really distraught, I don't know what I was going to do. It hits me that Tim is really, really gone, I'm not going to see or talk to him ever again. Right then SFC Ness called me, he had just left the funeral home in Arizona. He gave them Tim's class A's to send with Tim's body for his service back home. He also asked about Tim's funeral arrangements, the time, date, and location. He told me that Sgt. Marco and him will be flying down for Tim's service. Marco is another one of Tim's good friends who was also with the unit.

I was getting ready for bed and my phone rang. I said hello and again no one answered. I thought it was another wrong number.

Today was the day we were going to see Tim and we were driving down the road on the way to the funeral home. My grandson pointed up to the sky and said, "Look Blackhawk helicopters!" There were two Blackhawk helicopters hovering above us and they were still with us as we were almost at the funeral home. Another angel sign—Tim was with us.

At the funeral home I told Jerry what just had happened. He told us two helicopters flew over the funeral home a few minutes ago. Now I wondered if the funeral home had somehow arranged for this to happen, they knew about Tim being a Blackhawk crew chief and his love of flying. The next couple of weeks and the next two years proved me wrong, they were truly angel signs.

We were leaving the funeral home, very distraught, with the reality of Tim being gone. We heard bells and I thought we were standing too close to the door. We moved away believing that there was a sensor on the door so the funeral directors would know when someone entered the funeral home. We went to stand by our car, talking and crying while the bells were still ringing. By this time I was upset and annoyed by the ringing of the bells and said, "Where is that coming from?" We were looking around trying to see where the noise was coming from. Colin, my grandson, said that it was Uncle Tim getting his wings. There is an old saying "every time you hear a bell, it is an angel getting his wings." When my grandson said that we started really crying and saying that yes, it was Tim getting his wings. We felt comforted after that. It was amazing how God can use children to help comfort us in our most difficult times. We went home feeling much better. My grandson was our little angel comforting us.

Pete had arrived from Arizona. He was very shaken up. He stayed with Dan, they bonded and became very close. It turned out that Tim and Pete had gone way back. When Tim first moved to Arizona they had lived in the same apartment complex. We told Pete how grateful we were to him for staying with Tim and holding pressure on his wound, and how comforting it was to us for Tim to know help was on the way and that the person helping him was a good friend, someone he knew.

The day of Tim's visitation everyone commented on how good he looked. Even the people who had not met him mentioned how handsome he was. I agreed that I had a very good-looking family, both my children and grandchildren. The American flag was draped on his casket and he had his class A's on with all of his ribbons for his accomplishments. So many people were there. Tim was loved by many, many people. SFC Mike and Sgt. Marco arrived to the visitation and I met them for the first time. It felt like I known them for all of my life. They had said that Tim was like family and that now I was family. They said that they were never going away, that they were friends for life. They told me that they were going to have a memorial service for Tim in Arizona as well. Tim's visitation was beautiful, as was his funeral the next day.

In my prayers I asked God to tell Tim that I was going to give him a beautiful service with military rites and beautiful flowers. The colors red, white, and blue—red roses, white baby's breath and blue forget-me-not flowers—representing the military and big bright sunflowers. Tim used to eat sunflower seeds all the time as a child.

Many people had also sent flowers and plants, Marco had asked me if he could take pictures and I said yes. I imagined he was going to use them for the memorial service in Arizona.

When the service was over, we all went over to my nephew Mike's house and shared stories about Tim.

Marco gave me a CD and told me Tim's crew members and the rest of his unit had made a tribute to Tim. We watched it, loved it, and decided to add it on to his funeral service the next day. Marco did an excellent job on the CD.

Then it was the day, the day we said goodbye to Tim.

Tim's funeral was about to start and as the memorial video of Tim's life was on the big screen, the one that was shown at his visitation, "Amazing Grace" was playing in the background. We were viewing Tim for the last time before we closed the casket and said a prayer.

Pastor Jim Probst of Eastview Christian Church started the service speaking of Tim and how he wished he had known Tim, that everyone had spoken so highly of Tim. He said "I was told Tim was not afraid to die."

Several people went on to talk of Tim. Ron (RJ), his cousin, spoke about his "big life," he had gone places and done things people don't even experience in their lives of many more years. He had a great smile, a big smile, and he would tell us about the stories of his adventures.

His Aunt Millie talked about watching Tim and Dan while I worked and how kids, as some children do, get on parents nerves at times. We would call each other and say, "Want to do the switch-a-roo?" Meaning Dan or Tim would go to her house overnight and Mike or Ron would come to my house. Millie's boys, Mike and Ron, were the same age as Tim and Dan. They were all very close cousins. Tim's Aunt Cindy spoke of how she and Tim would play darts at a local bar and grill, The Windjammer, where Susie, another cousin of Tim's worked. She went on to say Tim would let her beat him at darts. He would go on and ask her if she wanted anything to eat, then let Susie know, and tell her to put it on his tab. He was like that with everyone; anytime you were out with Tim, bowling, dinner, playing darts he always wanted to pay.

Tim's distant cousin Jane had talked about when Tim was in Iraq, a classroom of students had a project to write a letter to a solider. Tim's name was given, so they wrote to him. Much to the kids' delight, Tim wrote back. They were so excited that a soldier was writing to them. Taylor, Tim's niece, talked about the club she and Uncle Tim created. It was called the "T" club which is what they both had in common. Their names both started with a "T" and they were both the oldest sibling. Dan had talked about how Tim had been a role model to him and how Tim had helped him when he was at his lowest point in his life; how humble, kind and generous he was.

Pete spoke of Tim, and of how he considered Tim his best friend. After he said those words he could not say anymore. He just cried.

Sgt. Mike Ness spoke of how Tim was a good solider,

I spoke of how wonderful Tim was and how he had always put everyone first before himself. I spoke of how Tim never liked to be called "Timmy," only special certain people like his Aunt Cindy could call him that. A few people chuckled and I said that we had just found out all of Tim's military unit including Sgt. Mike called him "Timmy." They didn't know, but I don't think Tim minded it at all. He loved his unit and enjoyed working with them.

I continued to speak of how I didn't eat, sleep, or shower for three days, I prayed that God would show me a sign that Tim was in heaven, I knew Dan and I and the kids knew. I wanted to let the rest of Tim's family and friends know. I expressed how I was concerned that I had not received a sign yet and how I prayed to God and said your son Jesus rose from the grave in three days, it has been four days. You are late. I told them how we did get our sign, at the end of the church service, on the big screen was a young man kneeling before Jesus. Jesus had his arms wrapped around him and an angel was behind them holding a white robe. I told everyone that I didn't know how I would have gotten through this without the signs we witnessed, the bells that rang, the helicopters, I addressed everything we had seen and heard. God was truly with our family during our most difficult time.

Sgt. Marco introduced the military tribute CD for Tim he had put together. We played it for Tim's service and it was a beautiful tribute. The song on the CD was Amazing Grace, the same song we chose for Tim's service. As the video was playing, arrangements were being prepared for Tim's military rites.

As Tim's casket was being rolled outside, everyone followed. The American flag still draped over his coffin, the rites began. The twenty-one gun salute began with the honor guard and SFC Ness and Sgt. Marco saluting Tim. Once the twenty-one gun salute was finished the flag was removed from the casket and the honor guard folded it.

They brought it to me and saluted me, thanking me for Tim's service in the United States Armed Forces. SFC Mike and Sgt. Marco were saluting during the whole ceremony. Tim's service was beautiful—I wanted to honor Tim. SFC Mike said Tim was probably looking down from heaven and saying, "What all this for me?" That's the type of person Tim was—very humble.

SFC Mike and Sgt. Marco left the following day. They had stopped by Tim's favorite bar and grill with Dan and the kids for lunch. They met Susie, Tim's cousin. They were shown where Tim played darts and shared memories with Susie. They had a beer in Tim's honor.

A few days later, I was at my sister Millie's house. I had another week and a half before I returned to work. My phone rang—I said hello and no one was there. I thought it might have been my brother Bobby calling, he had left me a couple of messages. I told Millie I needed to call him. Then she told me, "I remember you saying you felt like you were going to lose one of your children. Do you think God was preparing you?" I started thinking about it and said, "without that and signs he has been giving me, I don't know how I would be handling his death."

Millie and I decided to make dinner. Her son Ron, RJ, came over. RJ and Tim were only ten days apart in age. Millie and I did not plan it, that's just how it happened, and it was nice. They grew up together.

RJ brought his mom over an electronic device that played music you can upload, I forgot what it was called, but anyways RJ was explaining to his mom how it worked. RJ visited with us for a while as we again thought of Tim and shared memories.

Later that night Millie and I heard a loud beeping sound. We were in the family room—our ears following where the beeping sound was coming from in the house. It was in the living room, it is the device RJ brought over. Millie was trying to find out where you turn it off, I say just unplug it, Millie followed the cord, it was unplugged, and we looked at each other—it was still on. We both had a perplexed look on our faces, then I realized batteries. We couldn't find a place for batteries, and as the beeping continued Millie called RJ to ask him how to stop this beeping sound. She asked where the batteries compartment was.

RJ told his mom that there was no battery compartment. We both looked at each other. The beeping stopped.

I spent the night with Millie and the next day I went home. As I was pulling in the drive, I heard a helicopter. I looked up at the sky as I got out of my car. It was a Blackhawk helicopter, just like the ones we have seen at the funeral home and hovering over us on the road. I looked up and thought, "Was that you Tim? Last night at Aunt Millie's?" I went inside after the helicopter flew out of sight. I went out on my patio to water my flowers. My neighbors across the way were sitting on their patio enjoying the beautiful weather we were having.

They asked me, "Diane, did you see that Blackhawk helicopter?" I told them yes and they told me that they have lived there for ten years and have never seen a Blackhawk helicopter. With that, I had tears in my eyes. I knew that it was Tim, an angel sign from God, telling me when I see a Blackhawk it would be Tim looking out for me, and that he was always going to be with me.

Later that day my phone rang. It was SFC Mike Ness, he told me that they were planning Tim's memorial service. He said it was going to be a big deal, and that they were going to have it at Russell Auditorium, which is a popular venue for the military. He was going to send me the invitation that they made. It was to be held June 14th, 2013 at 1:00 p.m. We also talked about Tim's belongings, which were safely in storage on the base. Tim's unit and Pete had packed up his belongings.

We talked about the visit that I would have to make in the following few months, which was not a pleasant one. I thought about Tim a lot. I was glad to be going back to work soon, I felt I needed to keep busy. I remembered my niece was going to have a birthday in the next couple of days. She lived out of town. I needed to get her a card and send it off. I was at the dollar store looking at cards when my phone rang. I looked at it and it was all black. I thought, "What again? Wrong number?" But it was not lit up like someone was trying to call me. This had happened three or four times in the last two weeks. Then all of the sudden, I had this thought that it was Tim calling me back. I remembered the times I called Tim and then when realizing that Tim was not going to answer, I would hang up quickly. I started crying in the store. The clerk asked me if I was okay and I said that yes, I would be. I bought Lauren's birthday card and left the store.

I realized that this was also a sign, that it was Tim letting me know that he knew I was trying to call him. I told Dan this and he told me, smiling, that I should have said hello! We both knew it was Tim, and from that point on my phone has never done that again.

I was looking forward to going back to work the next day. Maybe things could get back into a routine again and feel normal. SFC Mike called again to let me know that they were going to make a CD of Tim's service there and add it onto the military tribute that was played at Tim's funeral. He said Sgt. Marco was putting it all together and, by the way, wasn't it time that I and my family started calling them Mike and Marco? We are family, that's right. I said you were Tim's family in Arizona—his military family.

At work everyone welcomed me back. It was nice to be back at work. My coworkers sent flowers, plants, and money to me. They were awesome. One coworker, Pam Wittenberg, had asked me if I had a flag box for Tim's flag. I had not gotten one yet. Later, I found out why she asked me that question, her husband Michael makes flag boxes. They surprised me with a beautiful custom flag box for Tim. It was big enough for the flag, Tim's cap, all of his ribbons, and a photo of him.

Made by Michael Wittenberg Pontiac, Illinois.

After a couple of months we were making plans for our trip to Arizona. We had witnessed a few more angel signs. Dan went to a local restaurant for take-out and when he got home on one of the soup lids it was marked Timm's. One day Dan was looking for garden ornaments for his yard. He found a white angel and on this angel was a turtle looking up at it. He bought it.

A friend came home for a visit. We were in a greenhouse outdoors looking at plants and flowers. I told her to listen because I heard a helicopter. We were outside and sure enough a Blackhawk helicopter was in the sky above us. She said, "Wow, you have a good ear." I think from the helicopters I have seen and heard, I can hear them from a mile away.

We got ready to go to Arizona to talk to the prosecutor and to bring Tim's personal belongings home. Once again, I was at my sister Millie's house, nervous about the trip. We talked and visited for a while. We spoke of Tim, then we noticed a camouflage Jeep driving right by her house. It passed right by her living room window. We looked at each other and Millie waved and said, "Hi Tim."

By this time these angel signs really comforted us. It reminded us that Tim was still with us. On our first trip to Arizona we were there to take care of personal business of Tim's. Pete met us at the airport. We wanted to see where this happened. We stopped by a flower shop and wanted to purchase a smaller bouquet of the flowers than we had at Tim's funeral service back home. We were at a stoplight waiting to turn into the flower shop. It was a red light. We were in two different vehicles waiting for the light to turn green, when I noticed on a pole there was a sign that read "TIM" in the upper right-hand corner. We were in the flower shop and I asked Dan, "Dan, did you see-" and immediately he said, "Yes, mom, I saw TIM on that sign." Dan was with Pete in his truck behind me and his dad. On a later trip to Arizona, I saw these signs through Mesa to Tempe, Arizona. We were traveling on the light rail to Tempe. As it turned out they were eco-friendly advertisements for what I believe is a utility company. We couldn't read the signs very well, as we were moving too quickly.

Every sign we see has the TIM on the upper right side of the sign, it's funny how we just saw one sign like that on our first visit, and the location was right where we were going to turn in the flower shop.

Once we were in the flower shop, we purchased the same arrangements of flowers with an American flag ribbon, but we couldn't find a sunflower. We asked the clerk if they had any, he looked and looked and we were about ready to give up when another clerk suggested going in the back cooler to look. There he found one sunflower, it was the only one left at the shop—another angel sign.

Tim was at the wrong place at the wrong time. He and another man were both stabbed, but the other man survived. As Tim ran outside he saw his friend Pete. Pete heard Tim yell "Pete, I've been stabbed!" Pete held pressure to Tim's wound while they were waiting for the police and ambulance. At that very spot, we placed the flowers.

Pete didn't know that was the last time he was going to see Tim.

We were only going to be in Arizona a couple of days and there was a lot to be done. Tim's car was coming home on a truck that hauls cars. His personal finances were taken care of with the help of Lt. Amanda Birch who also is with unit. She told us "Timmy" was her first crew chief when she first became a pilot. She loved flying with him.

Mike, Marco, Pete, along with some other guys from the unit had moved Tim's belongings from a storage unit to the base in anticipation of our arrival. They packed everything for us also.

The next morning we had an appointment to see the prosecuting attorney. He, along with Detective Brown, assured us that justice would be served. They said that it may take up to two to five years. That was very hard to hear. There were a lot of cases on the court's calendar. After the meeting, he assured me that he would keep me up to date and I could continue to call him or his assistant any time. They had been and continued to be very supportive.

We were at the military base, it was Labor Day weekend so most of the guys weren't there. SFC Mike gave us Tim's file. His military career was contained in all of those pages. The last few days had been overwhelming. Sgt. Ness offered to keep Tim's belongings on the base. He said, "Diane, you don't have to send them off now, take your time, they will be there when you are ready."

I remember the last time I was in Arizona. It was a fun time, I loved being there, but I didn't like it this time. I was so depressed and I just wanted to go home.

A year had passed since we had lost Tim and we were still waiting for justice to be served. The past year had contained many angel signs—my sister Linda from Colorado called me and told me she was on her patio, looked up in the sky and thought she saw Tim and Dawn's faces in the clouds. They were right next to each other. Dawn, Linda's daughter, had passed away at a young age also.

Blackhawk helicopters still fly over my condo, not as often, but it is nice when I see one. It really comforts me. The first Christmas without Tim was very hard. Tim was supposed to be home with us. I didn't want this to ruin our Christmas, I just wanted Tim with us. I bought lots of Christmas gifts to carry on Tim's generous spirit. Needless to say Dan had the same idea, we all received lots of gifts, most of them from Tim and the kids receiving gifts from Uncle Tim. I found a solider nutcracker that I am going to put him under the tree every year. I found a photo frame that reads, "Our Christmas Angel." I am doing the same with that, putting Tim's photo in it, alongside a personalized candle Millie gave me. I light it and say a prayer every Christmas, Veteran's Day, Fourth of July, Memorial Day, Flag Day, and Tim's birthday. These are going to be new traditions, including cake and ice cream for his birthday.

On Tim's birthday, we went out to eat. The waitstaff announced that there was a birthday in the house. They sang happy birthday and we sang along and quietly said Tim's name. It was so neat, it was like God was saying, "Hey, we are going to sing happy birthday because it is Tim's birthday." I said to Dan, "Yes, there is a birthday in the house. Tim was with us," even though the song was for another customer in the restaurant.

This past year there have been several angel signs. These signs have been very comforting. I will never forget the day I saw Tim. Another angel sign, it was a few months after Tim had passed away. I was at the beauty shop waiting to get my haircut while I was waiting for a hairstylist, I saw Tim, he walked right past the window, my eyes followed him until I could no longer see him. I got up from my chair, went to the door, went outside. I could no longer see him. He had passed by slowly. It was

Tim's profile, he had on a green T-shirt, his green army T-shirt that he worn under his army fatigues. I will never forget that, I remember this like it happened yesterday, how he walked past the window so slowly. The shop had a long window, it seemed like he wanted me to see him. I did see him, I couldn't believe it, I was completely in awe.

I knew that there was more business to attend to. Mike and I had been keeping in touch during the past year. I realized I was ready to send for the rest of Tim's things. I called Mike and let him know. He told me that he would make arrangements and call me the following week to give me the details. Mike then asked me how many of the CD's I would like that Marco was going to make copies for me. He also added the cookout they had in Tim's honor. The CD he was talking about was the tribute to Tim that they brought to his service plus the Memorial Service they had for him in Arizona and now a cookout in his honor. I couldn't wait to see the completed CD.

Dan was doing better, but he had his ups and downs. I'm sure the loss of his brother effected him. I knew he was mourning for his brother. I was afraid of how he was handling it and hoped he stayed strong. He continued going to church, which I was very thankful for, but he still had his moments of destructive behavior.

Mike called me to tell me that Tim's things were going to be home the next Monday. I happened to be off of work that Monday and Tuesday and was glad to have those days to go through his things and sort everything out. Tim's spirit had been with me this past year, and now the rest of Tim was coming home. He would no longer be in Arizona although his spirit might be—the 2-285 Kyotes have a memorial wall for Tim at their unit at Papago Park Military Reservation. Tim was coming home, coming home for good to Bloomington-Normal, Illinois.

As I was going through Tim's things, I remembered so many memories. It was very emotional, but I knew that I needed to do this. I found the St. Christopher chain I gave him when he was first deployed—The Saint of Safety. He had an Atlanta Braves poster—I remembered seeing that and teasing Tim, telling him that he was supposed to be a Cubs fan.

Tim was a huge collector of Budweiser Clydesdale memorabilia. I was so touched he kept everything I ever sent him. A Clydesdale Brewery stein, a US Army stein and a "Birth of a Nation" stein, along with mirrors, the Clydesdale White House provision mirror, and when Tim became a sergeant, I found his personalized Budweiser Mirror that read "Proud to serve those who have served us Sgt. Simpson." I found all of Tim's medals he had received for all of his accomplishments, with certificates along with them. Since I have Tim's flag box with his ribbons, I had a shadow box made for his medals and gave that to his dad. Dan has the White House provision mirror. The steins are kept in a curio cabinet along with the other treasures Tim held dear.

I wanted to keep Tim's spirit alive. I decided to give

The Windjammer in Bloomington, Illinois the mirror that reads, "Proud to serve those who have served us." The mirror is hanging above the dart board where Susie, Tim's cousin, put it. I thought that was the perfect spot for it. Kathy, the owner, agreed.

Tim's Atlanta Braves poster was given a big Atlanta Braves fan. I wanted something good to come from this awful tragedy. I gave my employer, OSF St. Joseph Medical Center, a gift of money. Much to my surprise they made a plaque of Tim, it still hangs in the surgical waiting room. Tim had passed away while in surgery. I snapped a picture of the plaque and sent it to Mike, along with the mirror at The Windjammer, something more to add to their memorial wall in Arizona. There is a little bit of Tim in Arizona and now also in Bloomington. I want his spirit to live on at both places.

Once the VFW Post 434 receive a glass case—which is being made—Tim's Blackhawk helmet, boots, US Army fatigues, and photos of the 285th Kyotes and Tim next to a U-60 Blackhawk helicopter will be given to them. I will send a photo of that to Arizona also.

As I was finishing up going through Tim's belongings, I found a lot of paperwork, most of it military paperwork. As I sorted through it I find papers Tim had written when he was in school, among them a paper entitled "Miracle Man." After I read it, I knew what I had to do.

• • • • •

TIM SIMPSON
CREATIVE WRITING
KUGLICH 1.1

MIRACLE MAN

"I can't believe this!" Libby whispered. "Am I the only one here that even cares?"

"Hush down, Libby. It's almost over and there will be food after the funeral," Steve whispered."

"Food? We're standing here in the pouring rain at my mother's funeral, and all you can think about is food? Steve, I'm sorry, but you obviously don't understand how I feel, and if you did, you wouldn't be thinking about food, especially at a time like this."

Steve gently grabbed Libby and held her. "I'm sorry It's just that I have a lot of things on my mind, and sometimes I get mixed up and don't set my priorities right. Look, Libby you know that I care and I'm really sorry that your mother died. I know that she ment a lot to you, but things change and we must go on, even without your mother. We'll always remember her."

"I know. I'm sorry, but everything seems unfair. She was so young. She had a good life and it ended so soon." Libby said as tears rolled down her cheeks. "I just don't

understand why God had to take her away so soon. I'd give anything to have her back, Steve, anything."

"I know," Steve whispered. "It's almost over, then we can go home."

"O.K." Libby said, "but this rain sucks and it doesn't make me feel any better." Saying nothing more, both Steve and Libby moarn the lost of her mother and waited until the funeral is finally over.

Afterward the rain had almost stopped and the sun had come out like it was the beginning of a bright new day.

"Steve," Libby said, "Doesn't it seem weird that it was just raining, and now it's sunny?"

"Not really," Steve said.

"I kind of thought that it did. Like God is happy that its all over," Libby said.

"Maybe he is."

"Whoa!" Both Libby and Steve shocked that someone was overhearing their conversation.

"Who are you? I don't know you. You shouldn't be here," Libby demanded.

"I'm a friend of your mothers, or was," the stranger said calmly. "I'm sorry for what happened to your mother, she was a good woman."

"Thank you," Libby said. " I appreciate your coming to her funeral. Now if you'll excuse us, Steve and I have to go home." As Steve and Libby headed toward the car, Libby really didn't quite know who the stranger was or how he knew her mother. All she knew was that he was kind of weird, and she didn't want to have anything to do with him.

" I could bring her back!" the stranger said.

"Excuse me," libby said. Getting very upset that the stranger had wasted more time then she had wanted.

"Listen mister, I don't know who you are or what you want, but you better leave right now!" Steve said.

"But I could bring her back," The stranger said hopefully once again.

After hearing this, Libby began crying again, remembering her mother and all the good times that they had together.

"O.K." Steve said. "I think its about time that you left. You are no longer welcome here. I think you should leave now!"

The rain started again, and the sun ran away. The clouds started to form, and the rain came as quickly as it went away. The stranger started to walk away saying once again that he could bring Libby's mother back from the grave.

"Alright!" Libby shouted. "Do it. If you can really bring her back from the grave, you have to prove it."

"O.K." The stranger whispered. Then without a second thought and a gesture with his hands he brought back Libby's mother from the grave.

"Oh my God," Steve screamed. Terrified of what had just happened. He grabbed Libby and tried to comfort her. Once again, tears began flowing down the sides of her cheeks. She turned toward the stranger and started to curse him.

"What did you do? Why?" Libby shouted.

"I did what you wanted me to do," The stranger whispered. "I brought her back from the grave."

"But," Libby whispered as tears rolled down her cheeks. "But she's still dead."

Still some but this is every a good story!!

45/50

• • • • •

This was another "angel sign." I was going to write a book about all of the angel signs we experienced. Many people had suggested that to me when I had told them about these signs, "You should write a book!" After reading that paper I decided that I was going to write a book. We are nearing the second year since we lost Tim. Taylor is getting ready to graduate from Normal West Community High School. Not only will her Uncle Tim not be at her graduation but her dad won't be either. Taylor is an excellent student, was on the homecoming court, and misses her Uncle a lot. They were in the "T" club. I felt so bad for her, I wanted to give her an extra special graduation gift.

Dan has not done well this past year, not only has he been drinking, he has been gambling, and lost all of the money Tim left him. When he hit rock bottom he finally decided to try rehab again. This time it was not in our town, he went to another town away from home that has a longer inpatient program. Hopefully he will complete this program.

I knew he was serious about the program when he did not leave the program to attend Taylor's graduation. Taylor was sad he wasn't there, but she knew it was best for her dad to stay where he was. He could not leave or communicate with anyone the first thirty days. Many times before Dan left rehab before the thirty days. We all wanted him to complete the program. With him being further away from his enablers maybe he would finish the program this time.

The day Taylor graduated, I found the perfect gift. She opened her gift and put her hands on her mouth and said, "What!" and began crying. I knew she loved it. It was her Uncle Tim's high school diploma. Her school was celebrating their twenty year mark. Tim's diploma read, "Tim Simpson—Normal West Community High School." Twenty years prior Tim had graduated. Club "T"—something else Taylor and Tim had in common. Taylor keeps Tim's diploma right next to hers. Taylor's graduation party was a success. She seemed very happy. Little did anyone know the next day I would be in Arizona.

Dan received a call from the rehab program. They were ready for him, they had an available bed. As luck would have it, he left a couple of weeks prior to Taylor's graduation. The kids took their dad to rehab, Taylor drove. We had thought if he was driven there he would have no transportation to leave the program early. As they were traveling down the highway, they made a stop. They noticed a vehicle with the license plate: 4TIM TY. We had discussed with Dan many times about how Tim would feel about his behavior. Taylor took a picture of the license plate. It was like telling Dan to do this for Tim—an angel sign from Tim.

The next day, I was getting ready to go to Arizona with a friend. We arrived early in the evening and planned to be there for about three weeks. I thought that I would text Taylor and let her know that I was so glad she liked her gifts. She had also received a personalized throw blanket with her name, year, and school on it. I would have to text her and Cheyenne for the next couple of weeks so they would think I was still in Illinois. If they wanted to get together, I would have to give them some kind of excuse why I couldn't.

Their dad had been in rehab only for a couple of weeks. For the first thirty days he could not communicate with anyone. I didn't want to tell Taylor or Cheyenne, in case after the thirty days, Dan would leave rehab and want to come to Arizona, I did not want him there with his state of mind. I did not want him in jail in Arizona. I was afraid he would punch the man that did this to his brother in court.

We had angel signs in Arizona. We saw Tim's car driving down the street. It wasn't his, of course, as Dan had his car in Illinois. I thought Tim was with us there. It was going to be very hard to see the man who murdered my son.

I called Mike the next morning, he welcomed us to Arizona once again. He suggested we take in a Diamondback baseball game. We found a schedule and there was a game June 1st. The Diamondbacks were playing the Atlanta Braves. June 1st was the date I received the keys to my condo, my closing date. Tim gave me the down payment for the condo. I always considered him buying me the condo because if it were not for his gift, I would never have been able to buy a home. I lived paycheck to paycheck and wasn't able to save money. With the date of the game and who the Diamondbacks were playing, we knew we were going to that game. June 1st, 2015 and yes, Atlanta won—angel sign.

We tried to get out and sightsee some, but it was very stressful. One morning, my friend asked me to go out in the hall of the hotel and look on the window of the door and she asked me what I saw. I looked and told her it looked like an angel with a trumpet. We took a picture of it. My nephew called me to let me know that they were back from vacation. They live in Arizona. I spent time with them and my sister Judy, who is now in a long term facility. It was nice seeing her and spending time with her. Our transportation was the rail, so we went to Mesa and took the rail to Tempe. Tempe is where Tim lived when he first moved to Arizona. On the rail ride through Mesa to Tempe, I saw those signs where the TIM was in the right-hand corner, it was the same sign we saw on our first visit to Arizona.

We were waiting for a sentence date. I wanted to get that over with and go home.

We attended church while we were there. After a church service one Sunday, we stepped into the church's gift shop which had lots of religious trinkets, gifts and cards. I saw a turtle. I smiled and thought of Tim. My friend noticed something else. She pointed above the turtle, and there was a card that read, "Mom, you are my bright and shining star." I started crying.

I called the kids and everyone else to let them know that I was in Arizona. By this time, Dan could have communication with the outside world. He called me and I explained that I didn't want him to leave rehab. I told him that I didn't tell anyone because I was afraid it might get back to him by accident. I told him that his dad will be the first to know the outcome and then I will call him. While

Sgt. Timothy Simpson Phoenix, AZ

2-285th Kyotes Phoenix, AZ.

in Arizona, during my downtime, I tried to start this book. I got nowhere, and it took me four hours to write two pages. I decided to put it off for a while. Sgt. Mike and Sgt. Marco were also anxiously waiting for the date of the sentencing. They would be there.

The day arrived—June 24th, 2015. Justice was served.

I am back home now in Illinois. It has been about five months since I have been back from Arizona. A couple of times I have seen Blackhawks flying overhead. I don't see them as often, but I know Tim is still with me. At home, my second bedroom has been turned into Tim's room. It is very patriotic, with pictures everywhere of Tim, his unit, his flag box, all honoring Tim. The unit has sent pictures that I have hung also.

One night I was watching TV at home and there was a knock at my patio door. I looked and I looked again. I didn't get up from the couch. I say, "Tim, Tim, is that you?" He said, "Yes mom it's me." I said, "Really, is that really you?" As I'm looking at him, I wonder why doesn't he come in, I feel like I can't move, I can only talk. I can't believe what I am seeing.

"Yes, mom, it's really me," he says.
"Oh no, Tim, I'm in trouble."
"Why?"
"You are alive. I spent your life insurance money."
"That's okay, we won't tell anybody."

"No, Tim, we will, your family, friends—people would want to see you, they would be so happy you're alive. I'm happy you're alive!"

"That's okay, mom, we will keep this our little secret."

With that, I awoke, I was in my bed—it was a dream, it was so very real. I wondered if after I spoke with Tim I went to bed, but didn't remember going to bed.

It's been quite a while since I had angel signs, that was the last one, I know I may not get them as often as the first two years, but I know every now and then I will, at least I hope so. I would love to hear from Tim and see more angel signs. Sgt. Mike and I had talked about all these angel signs. I sure hope someday Tim sends Mike one.

Sgt. Ness called me and told me that they were getting deployed to Kosovo in southeastern Europe and would not be back until Thanksgiving of 2016. I told him to please be safe. Sgt. Mike said that if Timmy was alive he would be going with them.

I visited Tim's memorial page that Dan set up. I told Tim that his unit was being deployed again. I noticed that someone had visited Tim's page recently. It was Sgt. Mike Ness, who had written a message on his page on a social network online memorial.

"Here we are getting ready to go out the door again, this time without Sgt. Simpson. We will miss you always little buddy. Keep us safe, Timmy."

Today is May 30th, 2016. Memorial Day. As I have done the last two years, I've submitted a memorial tribute to Tim in our local newspaper "The Pantagraph," this year the date of his death was on Memorial Day, May 30th 2016.

Thank you to all the men and women in our armed forces who have served and who are currently serving. God Bless you all.

X

I had another dream. I heard Tim's voice, he said, "Mom there is someone I want you to meet." I saw a large hand, palm side up. In the palm there was a tiny baby. Tim says, "Mom this is Elizabeth." I didn't understand the dream, not until I told Dan about it.

Dan had said, "Mom, at the funeral I was going to say something but I didn't know if you knew. I never heard you talk about it."

I asked, "Talk about what?"

Dan said Tim and his wife Sarah lost a baby.

"What?" I said.

Dan said, "Sarah had a miscarriage."

I remember having a phone conversation with Tim about Sarah being in the hospital; Tim had told me she would be okay, she was admitted for "female issues". That was all that was said about it.

I then understood the dream. Dan had told me later he was driving in his car listening to the radio. The announcer said that the next song played was dedicated to Elizabeth.

Angels are all around us, and I think there will always be angel signs.

CPSIA information can be obtained
at www.ICGtesting.com
Printed in the USA
BVOW05*0124180417
481562BV00017B/73/P